THIRTY DARN GOOD PRAYERS FOR BUSINESS

Amy Lykosh, Bob Perry

MAKARIOS
PRESS

MAKARIOS PRESS

CONTENTS

INTRODUCTION

Over the last five years, the Workplace Prayer team has experimented with prayers for business.

What prayers seem most effective?

What prayers are so powerful that we notice if we skip them?

How do we pray, morning, day, and night, without burning out?

It is our pleasure to bring you these thirty favorite prayers as an overview.

Big picture, "Thy Kingdom come" prayers; appropriate warfare prayers; prayers from the scripture; prayers from the saints.

Thank you for your interest in praying for businesses—we are excited for you to enjoy the best of what we've found across tens of thousands of hours.

CHAPTER ONE

PUSH THE RESET BUTTON

"For the Son of God, Jesus Christ, who was preached among you was not 'Yes' and 'No,' but in him it has always been 'Yes.' For no matter how many promises God has made, they are 'Yes' in Christ. And so through him the 'Amen' [the yes!] is spoken by us to the glory of God."[1]

All the promises of God are yes and amen!

Bob once proclaimed and prayed this prayer over business leaders.

***

The Lord says: push the reset button. Quit looking in the past. Quit looking at mistakes that you made.

---

1. 2 Corinthians 1:19-20

I have a major message of hope for you, and for others you serve.

Yes, you feel like the season of promise has passed you by, for your business, for your finances, and for your family.

But the answer is *NO*.

Our God is the God of the fifty millionth chance.

He gives you another chance. He wipes away shame, disappointment, and failure.

Things do go in seasons.

But the Holy Spirit is saying, "Push the reset button again."

Yes, look over those old promises.

Yes, look over those old prophecies.

Yes, look over those old dreams.

Yes, look over those old desires that have not been fulfilled yet.

And let your heart beat again with hope.

You can rise up because the Resurrected One lives inside of you.

As you push the restart button on your promises, and on your prophecies, and over your prayers, the Lord will fulfill the assignments for you.

***

Lord, we come together. It's been a battle for many of us. It feels like we've died to certain areas, desires, promises, prayers, passions.

But, Jesus, thank you that you breathe life.
We claim that life now.
And we push the reset button! Amen!

CHAPTER TWO

PRAYER WORKS

Almost the first day they met, Bob said to Amy: "Prayer works. Otherwise, why would we bother praying?"

Our prayers make a difference! God answers!

Think of the Lord's Prayer in Matthew 6:9-13 (KJV).

"Our Father which art in heaven, Hallowed be thy name."

This prayer begins with praise, but then transitions immediately into requests:

"Thy kingdom come, Thy will be done in earth, as it is in heaven."

An enormous first request: we want earth to look like heaven. Heaven has no injustice, no poverty, no pain, no miscommunication, no fear. Instead, it is so full of glory that the streets are paved with gold, and all the creatures worship the Lamb that was slain.

We can always pray for our lives and our work to be a picture of God's kingdom and will.

"Give us this day our daily bread."

So practical! And when the disciples asked for daily bread, they expected to have daily bread. They didn't wonder if maybe today they would go hungry when they asked.

No. They expected that when they asked, they would be satisfied.

We, too, can pray for the details, and expect answers.

"And forgive us our debts, as we forgive our debtors."

This prayer covers human relationships, and since business runs on relationships, this request is incredibly pertinent to business owners. It's a way of saying, "Keep us right before you and others. When others hurt us, may we not hold that against them."

"And lead us not into temptation, but deliver us from evil."

When we pray this, we expect that God is able to keep temptation and evil away from us, that God is strong enough to protect us.

"For thine is the kingdom, and the power, and the glory, for ever. Amen."

God owns the kingdom, and all power, and deserves all glory, both now and into eternity.

Prayer works.

Otherwise, why bother?

***

Jesus, thank you that in your prayer we find no sense of confusion, but only full confidence that this prayer will be efficacious.

Thank you that this is not some sort of theoretical, "wouldn't it be nice?" prayer, but rather an on-point, practical prayer, in which the disciples expected that you would answer their requests in power.

Lord, please give us that same sense of expectation that what we say to you matters. Thank you that when you speak, we get to speak back to you in faith, and that you are able to accomplish your plans through us.

Lord, we ask for an upgrade in understanding and ability, that you would be exalted in our lives, and that your name would be exalted in this earth.

In the name of Jesus, amen.

CHAPTER THREE

HEAVEN ON EARTH

The scripture tells us how to begin prayer: "Enter his gates with thanksgiving and his courts with praise; give thanks to him and praise his name."[1]

Jesus, too, in the Lord's Prayer, began with praising God's name: "Our Father, which art in heaven, hallowed be thy name."

Why do the scriptures insist on praise?

The next sentence in the Lord's prayer says, "Thy kingdom come, thy will be done on earth as it is in heaven."

In Revelation 4 and 5, we see a picture of heaven, where worship and praise flow constantly.

---

1. Psalm 100:4

When we enter his gates with thanksgiving and his courts with praise, we are bringing heaven to earth, fulfilling and satisfying the prayer that Jesus asked his followers to pray.

At least in this regard, we get to be the answer to our own prayers!

When we praise, we enjoy a bit of heaven on earth.

Praise remains one of the greatest weapons of warfare, removing heaviness and replacing it with the remembrance of the goodness and power of God.

***

Lord, we enter your gates with thanksgiving, and your courts with praise. Thank you for your presence with us. You are worthy of praise. Amen.

CHAPTER FOUR

THE SPIRIT OF WISDOM AND REVELATION

B ob teaches that, if we ever need to pray a prayer and we aren't sure what to pray, Ephesians 1:17 is always a great choice: "I keep asking that the God of our Lord Jesus Christ, the glorious Father, may give you the Spirit of wisdom and revelation, so that you may know him better."

The Ephesians 1:17 prayer brings insight and perception.

It's like night vision: it gives the ability to see more than what we know. It gives the ability to feel and discern.

Romans 14:17 says that the kingdom of God is righteousness, peace, and joy in the Holy Spirit.

Two out of three—peace and joy!—are feelings or emotions.

Part of the upgrade of Ephesians 1:17 is that we begin to recognize how God speaks to each of us individually, giving us supernatural intelligence, discernment, and wisdom.

In the daily fog of life, this prayer helps break through the cloudy conditions.

It's a storage bank into the necessary wisdom when we don't know what to do, where to go, when all else has failed.

Another translation: "I pray that the Father of glory, the God of our Lord Jesus Christ, would impart to you the riches of the Spirit of wisdom and the Spirit of revelation to know him through your deepening intimacy with him."[1]

Paul seeks to *impart* these riches: not only to communicate, but also to bestow, to give.

The infinite wise God desires to give us ideas. The infinite wise one, the Everlasting Father, desires to give us the plans, the book, the blueprint that will impact people's lives.

This prayer brings results now, but, in the beauty of God's abundance, it also offers long-term benefits, like a time release capsule.

This prayer is good any time, and in any season, but especially when you're starting something, or when your back's against the wall, or when you need breakthrough.

Pray big. God has plans and purposes that he wants to reveal to you.

Pray big. The spirit of wisdom and revelation is upon you.

---

1. *The Passion Translation*

***

Lord, may we walk with peace and confidence, even in the delays in our lives. Thank you for the partnership in intercession with the Holy Spirit, the divine helper, who reveals God's unfailing purposes. Thank you that we walk in God's love as his beloved joy.

Lord, we desire your wisdom and revelation, your knowledge and enlightenment.

Release your riches, Father of glory. Amen.

CHAPTER FIVE

LET YOUR REQUESTS BE MADE KNOWN TO GOD

S erial entrepreneur Paul Van Hoesen went to an executive retreat, and came back with a blessing.

***

Philippians 4:6 says something very simple: "Be anxious for nothing, but in everything by prayer and supplication, with thanksgiving, let your requests be made known to God."

The word "everything" truly means *everything*. Particularly in business.

In these days, the Lord is moving upon many hearts to make a dramatic impact—even in areas like the arts.

We had an incredible encounter at Sight and Sound Theater.

A Mennonite group has been raised up there, impacting the world through their art.

If you think the arts have been completely given over to the liberal world, you're mistaken.

There in Lancaster, Pennsylvania, they are producing stage productions so creative that even Disney comes and looks, because it's a new level.

And all of this is rooted in prayer.

If you're a business person, how absolutely critical it is to support the intercessors.

Support the prayer movement. Get people in your company praying specifically for what you're doing. And let's watch the Lord's breakthrough.

***

Lord, we thank you this day that you are speaking this word very loudly in the body of Christ, that businesses should be bathed in prayer.

We should be anxious for nothing, but in everything, by prayer and supplication, may we raise up intercessors and prayers to the Lord, to see the breakthroughs that we want to accomplish in the earth.

Lord, we want to accomplish great things for you, and that takes great prayer.

Lord, we pray: continue to stir our hearts, and bring it forth. In Jesus' name, amen.

CHAPTER SIX

BREAK OFF VOICELESSNESS

"Great crowds came to him, bringing the lame, the blind, the crippled, the mute and many others, and laid them at his feet; and he healed them. The people were amazed when they saw the mute speaking, the crippled made well, the lame walking and the blind seeing. And they praised the God of Israel."[1]

Even extremely articulate people can have a few thin slices of voicelessness.

"I can write a training manual, but I can't write a book."

"I can talk to friends, but I don't want to make calls."

"I hate public speaking."

And then there's the unstated but very real phenomenon of simply not being willing to pray aloud.

---

1. Matthew 15:30-31

Let's pray off voicelessness.

***

Lord Jesus, when you walked this earth, you healed the mute tongue.

Lord, when we come to you with a sense of voicelessness—"I don't know what to say, I don't know that my words are going to come out clearly, maybe everybody else is better than I am at speaking or praying, I will keep quiet"—Lord, thank you that you specialize in healing, and have no trouble healing voicelessness.

Lord, please go forth in power and release the mute tongue. Release worship and praise and prayer. Release speeches and books and the ability to speak truth to power (with love).

Lord God, cut us free of any fear or inferiority. Move in power.

In your precious name, Jesus, amen.

CHAPTER SEVEN

PRAYER OF PROTECTION

"Heal the sick, raise the dead, cleanse those who have leprosy, drive out demons. Freely you have received; freely give."[1]

Jesus gave these instructions to his disciples. Amy didn't grow up in a church tradition that thought much about demons. If anything, curses, hexes, and spells seemed as realistic as an animated movie.

But when she went through Francis MacNutt's *Deliverance* training, he said, "There are 63 active covens[2] in Jacksonville, Florida."

Covens target ministries and churches by name.

---

1. Matthew 10:8

2. a group of witches who meet regularly

At the time he said that, Jacksonville was a city of less than a million people.

Think of 63 regular gatherings seeking the downfall of the kingdom of God.

That's a lot of active resistance in a population.

The churches we attend, the ministries we serve, the businesses that glorify God: these face active resistance, people who are at enmity with God, and who target believers specifically.

This is not meant to be scary—what are the works of the enemy next to the matchless blood of Jesus?—but it is meant to be sobering.

Jesus gave instructions in the Lord's prayer: "Deliver us from evil" or "deliver us from the evil one."

And so we pray for protection against the works of the evil one.

Francis MacNutt's Christian Healing Ministries website includes the prayer of protection, below, which includes the line, *We bind up the powers of earth, air, water, fire, the netherworld and the satanic forces of nature. We break any curses, hexes or spells sent against us and declare them null and void.*

The author explained: "'Earth, air, fire, and water' are unfamiliar categories to most of us, but these are the main elements of the world as the ancients divided them. The reason we put them in the prayer are simply the categories that Satanists use in casting curses. For instance, demons that inhabit the 'air' can cause hurricanes. You need not use these categories, of course, if you had rather not. We are simply breaking curses by reversing them in the same terms that Satanists use."[3]

***

In the name of Jesus Christ and by the power of his Cross and his Blood, we bind up the power of any evil spirits and command them not to block our prayers. We bind up the powers of earth, air, water, fire, the netherworld and the satanic forces of nature. We break any curses, hexes or spells sent against us and declare them null and void. We break the assignments of any spirits sent against us and send them to Jesus to deal with them as he will. Lord, we ask you to bless our enemies by sending your Holy Spirit to lead them to repentance and conversion. Furthermore, we bind all interaction and communication in the world of evil spirits as it affects us and our ministry. We ask for the protection of the shed blood of Jesus Christ over _____.

Thank you, Lord, for your protection and we ask that you send your angels to help us in the battle. We ask you to guide us in our prayers: share with us your Spirit's power and compassion. Amen.

---

3. https://www.christianhealingmin.org/images/CHM/downloads/Prayerfor Protection2.pdf

CHAPTER EIGHT

CUTTING-FREE

B ob tells the story of his mentor Rosemarie Claussen. Her father was a high-ranking German military officer. The day she was born, her father went to work extra happy, and his superior officer asked why he was in such a good mood. "I have a daughter!"

"I'd like to be the godfather of your child."

That's how Rosemarie Claussen's birth certificate came to list the name of her godfather: Adolf Hitler.

She grew up with a deep sense of the importance of alliances.

Later, when Corrie ten Boom mentored Rosemarie, Corrie taught about the power of prayer to cut off alliances and connections.

We all need this teaching.

When we go through our day and interact with others, we form connections. We take on problems.

Some of that is, presumably, good. Scripture tells us in Galatians 6:2 to bear one another's burdens. But we're not supposed to carry these burdens ourselves. Let's bear those burdens to Jesus.

Perhaps the ideal would be that after every call, every meeting, every shopping trip, we would remember to pray a cutting-free prayer.

But ideally at least once a day.

When the disciples walked with Jesus, they got dusty and needed to be cleaned off.

"After that, he poured water into a basin and began to wash his disciples' feet, drying them with the towel that was wrapped around him."[1]

We, too, appreciate regular showers.

Sometimes Amy will catch herself: "I started off today so cheerful and enthusiastic. What went wrong?"

When she looks back over the day, usually she will remember an interaction that left her under a gray cloud.

Time for the cutting-free prayer![2]

***

Lord Jesus, thank you for sharing with us your wonderful ministry of healing and deliverance. Thank you for the healings we have seen and experienced today. We realize that the sickness

---

1. John 13:5

2. https://www.christianhealingmin.org/images/CHM/downloads/CuttingF reePrayer.pdf

and evil we encounter is more than our humanity can bear, so cleanse us of any sadness, negativity or despair that we may have picked up. If our ministry has tempted us to anger, impatience or lust, cleanse us of those temptations and replace them with love, joy and peace. If any evil spirits have attached themselves to us or oppressed us in any way, we command you, spirits of earth, air, fire, water, the netherworld and the satanic forces of nature, to depart—now—and go straight to Jesus Christ for him to deal with you as he will.

Come Holy Spirit: renew us—fill us anew with your power, your life, your joy, and your wisdom. Strengthen us where we have felt weak and clothe us with your light. Fill us with life. Lord Jesus, please send your holy angels to minister to us and our families—guard us and protect us from all sickness, harm and accidents. We praise you now and forever, Father, Son and Holy Spirit, and we ask these things in Jesus' Holy Name that he may be glorified. Amen.

CHAPTER NINE

THE ABILITY TO EXECUTE PLANS

The prophet said of Jesus: "The Spirit of the Lord will rest on him—the Spirit of wisdom and of understanding, the Spirit of counsel and of might, the Spirit of the knowledge and fear of the Lord."[1]

What a prophecy!

Amy once asked Bob, "Is it okay to pray for this for me? I don't want to overreach, since Isaiah said this of Jesus."

Bob said, "Paul said in 1 Corinthians 2:16 that we have the mind of Christ, and Jesus himself said in John 14:12 that we will do greater works than he did. So pray it for yourself! Absolutely!"

---

1. Isaiah 11:2

Well ... that blows open the doors of possibility!

Gilbert Hintz, a large-scale organic farmer, read this same verse in the New English Translation and adopted it as his life verse: "The Lord's Spirit will rest on him—a Spirit that gives extraordinary wisdom, a Spirit that provides the ability to execute plans, a Spirit that produces absolute loyalty to the Lord."

So often in business we have good ideas, but then we don't know how to execute them with excellence.

***

Lord, we need wisdom, far more than we have. Thank you for the promise in James 1:5 that we can ask with eager and confident expectation that you will give wisdom as often as we ask.

Thank you.

And, Lord, we want your extraordinary wisdom, combined with the ability to execute plans. Yes, Lord! Pour that out!

And we also want to be absolutely loyal to you, Lord.

Teach us your ways and let us walk in your will. May we be effective in your kingdom.

Thank you, Lord. In Jesus' name, amen.

CHAPTER TEN

BUSINESS BLESSING

"*T*he people curse him who holds back grain, but a blessing is on the head of him who sells it."[1]

This verse doesn't say, "The people bless those who give away the work of their hands."

No. The one who sells blesses the people.

Selling goods and services blesses the community. The willingness to be in business is a gift.

Another translation (KJV) reads, "He that withholdeth corn, the people shall curse him: but blessing *shall be* upon the head of him that selleth it."

A blessing shall be on the head of the salesperson, on the head of the business owner.

---

1. Proverbs 11:26

Other meanings of this word: a benediction, prosperity, the praise of God, a gift, a treaty of peace, the source of blessing.[2]

Not the prosperity gospel as "sow your seed and get a private jet," but, rather: sell what the people need, and receive a blessing, a benediction, prosperity.

Desire and expect a blessing in the work of your hands.

***

Lord, you offer business to your people as a way for your children to serve each other.

For all the righteous goods and services, for all those taking risks of buying and selling, we ask for your blessing, and for prosperity.

Amen.

---

2. https://www.blueletterbible.org/lexicon/h1293/kjv/wlc/0-1/

CHAPTER ELEVEN

THE LORD'S KIND PRESSURE

A my once sent this email and prayer.

***

I am in a season right now where I feel like every day or two, I need to have some form of healing prayer.

I had no idea that I had that many issues within that needed to be resolved! I continue to be astonished by how much additional healing the Lord has for me.

Things like: fear of failure. Certainty that I am not acceptable to God.

Sometimes, in past seasons of significant change, I have said to the Lord, "I think this rate of change is actually too much.

I'm too tired. I cannot handle this. Could we please slow it down a bit?"

And God is so gracious—he slows down the rate of change.

In this case, though, I have the margin to handle this change. Even so, I mentioned to a friend that, though I am grateful for the refining fire, I feel, at times, a bit flayed.

My friend is a seer, someone who sees visions. (I didn't even know this was a thing until recently, but it is. Some people hear from God. Some see visions. Some see visions more than others.)

She wrote:

> Amy, I saw the Lord pressing down on your heart, and some dross was coming up, and he was so comforting and tender with you. His pressure was intentional. His healing power present to deliver. But he was so unphased by what was coming out.
>
> Like it was just another day in paradise.
>
> He was so tender and joyful with you. Like a child that gets their tooth extracted and the parent is with them when they get happy gas. How the parent smiles at the drama and yet has so much compassion knowing what the child is facing.

This picture of the Lord putting pressure on me, and out comes some dross—I find it hilarious.

Like popping a pimple: it's not a big deal.

Like the Lord is saying, "I'm not worried about what is coming out of you, because I know what I'm putting in you and I know your heart."

This picture of Jesus was a soothing balm on all those tender places where he is molding and shaping me.

The Lord is at work, with affection and good cheer, and he's not worried about the process.

This picture isn't just for me and my journey.

It's how he sees you and your journey, too. Unphased by what comes out. Comforting and tender.

It's just another day in paradise.

***

Lord, in Philippians 1:6, Paul wrote, "Being confident of this, that he who began a good work in you will carry it on to completion until the day of Christ Jesus."

Lord, as you press on us, if dross comes out in the beginning, thank you that you are purifying us.

Thank you that you are able to complete the good work you began. Thank you that the process doesn't stress you out, that you don't wonder, "Maybe this time the plan I've made won't work out. Maybe this will be the one human I'm not able to help."

Thank you that you enjoy our growth, as a parent delights in a child's growth.

You're a good God, and it is our delight to serve you.

In Jesus' name, amen.

CHAPTER TWELVE

DISSOLVE DIFFICULTIES

T he world changes so quickly, we need to be able to see around corners. We need supernatural help to know what we have no way of knowing in the natural.

"Daniel, whom the king called Belteshazzar, was found to have a keen mind and knowledge and understanding, and also the ability to interpret dreams, explain riddles and solve difficult problems."[1]

Another translation says of Daniel: "Forasmuch as an excellent spirit, and knowledge, and understanding, interpreting of dreams, and shewing of hard sentences, and dissolving of doubts."[2]

He had an excellent inner man, an excellent spirit.

---

1. From Daniel 5:12

2. KJV

He had knowledge and insight. The building blocks of information, and the ability to use those wisely and well.

He had the ability to interpret dreams. The communication from God during sleep? He knew what those dreams meant.

He could explain riddles or puzzles, eliminating any confusion.

He could dissolve the difficulties. When faced with a knotty problem, he knew how to unwind it, or how to cut through.

We need these gifts in the work of our hands.

Understanding. Bigger picture thinking. The ability to know which pieces of information are important in this season, and which can be left aside. We need to be able to solve problems and unravel mysteries.

***

Lord, like Daniel, would you give us a keen mind and knowledge and understanding, and also the ability to interpret dreams, explain riddles and solve difficult problems. We need all of this and more in our business. Thank you. Amen.

CHAPTER THIRTEEN

ORDER OUT OF CHAOS

"Now the earth was formless and empty, darkness was over the surface of the deep, and the Spirit of God was hovering over the waters."[1]

Perhaps this verse means something like: "the Spirit hovered over chaos and darkness."

But in the context of ancient texts, this verse more likely means something like: "the Spirit hovered [brooded, incubated] over infinite possibility."

When we find ourselves in a swirl, may we think, "This is unrealized potential. What will God make of it?"

***

---

1. Genesis 1:2

Lord, in each situation, may we remember to be curious: "What will you do next?"

When we are in a good place: "What will you do next?"

When we are in a desperate place: "What will you do next?"

Lord, be at work in us! In our order and our chaos—which is really the infinite possibility, the unrealized potential!

Amen!

CHAPTER FOURTEEN

HEWING A PIONEER PATH AHEAD

A traditional translation of Luke 2:52: "And Jesus grew in wisdom and stature, and in favor with God and man."

When New Testament scholar Kenneth Wuest translated the New Testament, his version of Luke 2:52 says: "Jesus kept on hewing a pioneer path ahead, making steady progress in wisdom, maturity, and favor in the presence of God, and with men."

There's a saying in business circles: "You can always tell who the pioneers are, because they have arrows in their back and are lying face down in the dirt."

When we try to take new territory, and feel like we're under attack all the time, the truth is that Jesus is, and always has been, the true pioneer.

He goes before us, and we walk in his footsteps.

He also protects our backs.

Before and behind.

"But you will not leave in haste or go in flight; for the LORD will go before you, the God of Israel will be your rear guard."[1]

"Then your light will break forth like the dawn, and your healing will quickly appear; then your righteousness will go before you, and the glory of the LORD will be your rear guard."[2]

***

Lord Jesus, thank you for forging a pioneer path ahead, and that the glory of the LORD is our rear guard.

Thank you that we don't ever walk alone, because you are with us.

---

1. Isaiah 52:12

2. Isaiah 58:8

Chapter Fifteen

PROSPEROUS PEOPLE

B ob once prayed this powerful prayer.

***

Lord, I kept hearing John's prayer in 3 John 2: "Beloved friends, I pray that you are prospering in every way, and that you continually enjoy good health, just as your soul is prospering."

Dear friend, dear sister, dear brother, I hope all is well with you, and that you are as healthy in body as you are strong in spirit.

Lord, we proclaim that our brothers and sisters, these men and women and their businesses and ministries, are beloved.

We pray that in every way they may succeed and prosper and be in good health physically, just as you know their souls are prospering spiritually.

We pray that our brothers and sisters will prosper in every way. We proclaim prosperity upon them in every way possible.

Lord, the King James says, "Beloved, I pray that you may prosper in all things, and be in health just as your soul prospers." We speak the life of God upon them.

The Message Bible says, "I pray for good fortune. I pray that the Lord will direct you in everything you do. I pray for your good health." I pray for health in your body, health in your soul, health in your relationships, that your everyday affairs prosper, as well as your soul.

We proclaim the voice of the Lord upon our brothers and sisters, we proclaim, oh God, your voice thundering, as in Psalm 29.

Beloved friends, we pray that everything is going well for you, and that your body is as healthy as your soul is prosperous.

We proclaim that they are in step with God, and under the divine protection of the Lord.

We extend the umbrella of God's protection upon each family represented. Each family and each family that they serve, whether through work, or through ministry. We pray for heaven's protection. Protect them physically, emotionally, spiritually, mentally. In Jesus' name, amen.

CHAPTER SIXTEEN

PROSPEROUS CITIES

W hen the people of Judah were taken captive to Babylon, Jeremiah wrote them these words:

> This is what the Lord Almighty, the God of Israel, says to all those I carried into exile from Jerusalem to Babylon: "Build houses and settle down; plant gardens and eat what they produce. Marry and have sons and daughters; find wives for your sons and give your daughters in marriage, so that they too may have sons and daughters. Increase in number there; do not decrease. Also, seek the peace and prosperity of the city to which I have carried you into exile. Pray to

theLord for it, because if it prospers, you too will prosper."[1]

When we look at our cities, we can see corruption and sin, injustice and evil. With all these problems, wouldn't God be more inclined to judge us than bless us?

God shows his perspective in the words of Jeremiah.

The Babylonians had been God's instrument of judgment on the idolatrous children of Israel, God's chosen people, the apple of his eye.

But the Babylonians were not righteous God-fearers.

The idolatrous children of Israel, in captivity to the unrighteous heathen.

And yet God tells the children of Israel: "Seek the peace and prosperity of the city to which I have carried you into exile. Pray to the Lord for it, because if it prospers, you too will prosper."

When your city prospers, you prosper.

Seek the *shalom* of your city, a Hebrew word that includes the ideas of completeness, safety, soundness, health, prosperity, welfare, peace, quiet, tranquility, contentment, friendship with man, friendship with God, absence of war.[2]

---

1. Jeremiah 29:4-7

2. https://www.blueletterbible.org/lexicon/h7965/kjv/wlc/0-1/.

***

Lord Jesus, when you came to the earth and saw the crowds, you taught them, healed them, blessed them, comforted them, corrected them (when needed). You loved them.

So, too, for us.

May we carry your comfort and compassion to our communities.

And, Lord, we recognize that thriving businesses make thriving cities.

Please bless our businesses to prosper. Amen.

CHAPTER SEVENTEEN

REMEMBER TESTIMONIES

"And they overcame him by the blood of the Lamb, and by the word of their testimony; and they loved not their lives unto the death."[1]

In Dutch Sheets' book *Giants Will Fall*, a Messianic Jewish rabbi explained the meaning of the Hebrew word for "testimony."

"The word doesn't mean simply to convey something from the past.... Its true meaning is 'to repeat an action or do it again.' We Hebrews believe ... that when we share about what God in the *past*, it releases the same power into the *present* ... in other words, power is released to 'do it again.'"[2]

---

1. Revelation 12:11 (KJV)

2. p. 60

Jews share the stories of the Old Testament so that those stories can be released today.

To share a testimony doesn't just mean "remember," but includes a request to "*do* what is being thought about."

When God says in Isaiah 43:26, "Put me in remembrance," he doesn't need a reminder, as if he forgot.

"Rather, He is instructing us to ask Him, based on something said or done in the past, to take action today."[3]

We remember testimonies as a prayer to ask God to do it again.

***

Lord, would you bring to mind a story that encouraged us.

A friend's cancer treatment that worked. The new product launch that hit. The last minute miraculous provision, that covered the need to the penny. The team that persevered through incredible odds to find success. The partnership that dissolved at the right time, and in the right way. The tech issue that eventually resolved. The bureaucratic red tape that evaporated.

As we face challenges, remind us of the different testimonies. "Do it again, Lord, for me."

You are faithful, and if you did something once, you can do it again.

Please do.

---

3. p. 61

CHAPTER EIGHTEEN

EXPECTATION OF HARVEST

"**D**o not be deceived: God is not mocked, for whatever one sows, that will he also reap."[1]

The Lord established the principle of sowing and reaping. When farmers sow seeds, they expect them to grow and produce a harvest.

And just because sometimes the locusts come, or tornadoes, or fire ... if the principle of sowing and reaping didn't work most of the time, we would have starved long ago.

Usually, the law of sowing and reaping actually works. We don't think about it much, though, because no newspaper reports, "Grocery stores have food again today! Go buy what you need!"

---

1. Galatians 6:7

But one of the ways the enemy distorts our thinking is that we start to doubt whether what we do has any sort of result.

Or we focus on all of the times that we planted something and the raccoons came and dug them up, or we planted crops and the bugs came and ate them. Rather than focus on what works, we focus on what doesn't.

***

Lord Jesus, you walked the earth as a righteous man. But you went to the cross—hardly a reward of righteousness.

On the other hand, from the larger perspective, you are now seated at the right hand of the Father, and we know that every knee will bow.

So even with your unjust death, you sowed and will reap.

Lord, let us see the bigger picture of how the law of sowing and reaping actually works.

In a garden, sometimes tender plants freeze, and others don't produce much.

Similarly, sometimes in the Spirit, we plant through prayer and testimonies. We teach our children and live with intentionality.

And yet these seeds don't seem to grow, or they don't multiply in the timeframe that we're expecting, or in the ways that we had hoped.

Lord, increase our faith. Remind us that you established sow-ing and reaping, springtime and harvest, and that, in you, the work we are doing will not be worthless.

Let us press in to believe for a harvest.

And we pray that you would make us attentive. May we recount your good deeds, as in Psalm 103: you forgive our sins and heal our diseases, and so on. And you go above and beyond, as Ephesians 3:20 says: you are "able to do immeasurably more than all we ask or imagine, according to his power that is at work within us."

Thank you, Lord. We love you. Amen.

CHAPTER NINETEEN

HOW TO ASK FOR WISDOM

"**I**f any of you lacks wisdom, you should ask God, who gives generously to all without finding fault, and it will be given to you. But when you ask, you must believe and not doubt, because the one who doubts is like a wave of the sea, blown and tossed by the wind. That person should not expect to receive anything from the Lord. Such a person is double-minded and unstable in all they do."[1]

When James says, "you must believe and not doubt," he doesn't mean "you must have faith that God will give you wisdom, and not be uncertain about it, not question it."

Joshua Jagelman clarified that when Paul says, "you must believe and not doubt," the Greek word for "doubt" is *diakrino*. *Dia* means "passing through," with the sense of "a division

---

1. James 1:5-8

of two or more parts," and "krino" means "judgements." Two options, two opinions.

Joshua said, "God does not like being one of your options. And if you come to God so that you can add one more option to your strategies, you probably will not receive much from him. If I have a good strategy, but I ask God and he says something different, I'm going to have to do what he says."

When you ask, you must believe, *pistis*, "faith," and not decide between two options.

Do not add God's wisdom to the list and decide which action to pursue. Do not have multiple judgments that you decide between.

If you're wondering why you're not hearing from God, perhaps it's because you asked him for an option.

"The one who doubts is like the wave of the sea, blown and tossed by the wind. That person should not expect to receive anything from the Lord. Such a person is double-minded."

"Double-minded" is "dipsychos," or "twice" (*dis*) and "souled" (*psyche*)

The double-minded person has a heart for God, and a heart for the world.

In the Greek it's really clear: double, double, double.

If you want to have wisdom from God, don't add God to your list of options, and don't have a heart for the world.

If you do, do not expect to receive anything from God.

***

Lord God, thank you that we don't need to have a list of options, but that you give wisdom as we need it.

Remind us, Lord, to seek your kingdom first and only. Let us see your faithfulness so that we believe that all these things will be added as well. Thank you that when you went to make an oath, the only unchangeable thing you could find was yourself, and so you swore by yourself. Thank you that you forgive us and welcome us.

Keep us from a heart for the world. Let us turn our hearts to you fully.

Thank you for sending Jesus as our example, that he set his face like flint towards Jerusalem and his death, and that, through his death and resurrection, we have life abundantly.

Chapter Twenty

LOTS OF BLESSINGS

"Jabez cried out to the God of Israel, 'Oh, that you would bless me and enlarge my territory! Let your hand be with me, and keep me from harm so that I will be free from pain.' And God granted his request."[1]

Jabez asked for blessing and influence, for protection and comfort.

And the verse doesn't end with, "And God, angered, smote Jabez for asking for too many blessings."

No. Jabez prayed a big prayer, "And God *granted* his request."

---

1. 1 Chronicles 4:10

We can ask the Lord to bless us! Ask for more influence! Ask for protection![2] Ask for comfort!

We get to voice the desires in our heart.

We have permission to say to God, "This is what I want."

Though the prayer for expanded borders doesn't have to be a literal request, it can be one.

Some possibilities to pray for:

• Fame: "Do you see someone skilled in their work? They will serve before kings; they will not serve before officials of low rank."[3]

• Favor: "For those who find me find life and receive favor from the Lord."[4]

• Promotion: "Whoever pursues righteousness and love finds life, prosperity and honor."[5]

• Stocks to increase in value: "I form the light and create darkness, I bring prosperity and create disaster; I, the Lord, do all these things."[6]

• Wells and oil rights to multiply: "I will give you hidden treasures, riches stored in secret places, so that you may

---

2. As any investor knows, it's so terribly important not to lose the gains you've earned.

3. Proverbs 22:29

4. Proverbs 8:35

5. Proverbs 21:21

6. Isaiah 45:7

know that I am the Lord, the God of Israel, who summons you by name."[7]

• Gold, silver, gems and precious stones: "And I will make the Egyptians favorably disposed toward this people, so that when you leave you will not go empty-handed. Every woman is to ask her neighbor and any woman living in her house for articles of silver and gold and for clothing, which you will put on your sons and daughters. And so you will plunder the Egyptians."[8]

• Company greatness: "From the fruit of their lips people are filled with good things, and the work of their hands brings them reward."[9]

• Community value to go up: "Also, seek the peace and prosperity of the city to which I have carried you into exile. Pray to the Lord for it, because if it prospers, you too will prosper."[10]

In partnership with the Holy Spirit, what do you want to request?

As we are in partnership with God, he gives us desires, then sanctifies those desires, and finally satisfies them, too.

---

7. Isaiah 45:3

8. Exodus 3:21-22

9. Proverbs 12:14

10. Jeremiah 29:7

When we have the desire to pray for something, we get to do so in partnership with God. Our desires, as the Lord's covenant people, come about because of the Lord's will. The Holy Spirit is at work, as we work in collaboration with God.

***

"If only you would bless me, extend my border, let your hand be with me, and keep me from harm, so that I will not experience pain."[11]

Lord, extend my borders in all the ways that you invite me to.

---

11. 1 Chronicles 4:10 (Christian Standard Bible)

CHAPTER TWENTY-ONE

THE ABILITY TO PRODUCE WEALTH

O ne of the best prayers to pray over your business: "But remember the LORD your God, for it is he who gives you the ability to produce wealth, and so confirms his covenant, which he swore to your ancestors, as it is today."[1]

From its founding in 1990, the homeschool company Sonlight Curriculum offered morning prayer meetings, on the clock, for their staff.

Thirty years later, the owners hired Bob to pray.

Within a few months, they were amazed at the increase.

President Sarita Holzmann said, "For thirty years, we have prayed for our customers, for our staff, for our vendors, for

---

1. Deuteronomy 8:18

our materials, for the unreached peoples of the world ... but I never once thought to pray for increase."

But why wouldn't the Lord want to bless his children with increase?

As business owners, and as people of prayer, we want to pray for all the blessings the Lord has for us.

***

Lord, thank you that your word says that you are the one who gives the ability to produce wealth. We're asking for financial increase. Your word says this, so as one of your children, seeking to make a difference in your kingdom, please do what you say.

Lord, confirm the covenant.

Expose the things that need to be exposed in order to drive out unrighteousness. Lord, for your righteous ones, bring clarity, direction, and purpose.

May we be productive in your kingdom, for your name's sake.

CHAPTER TWENTY-TWO

SEATED IN THE HEAVENLY REALMS

W hen someone is grumpy around us, it's easy to match their grumpiness. If someone speaks out of frustration, it's easy to feel our own frustration level rise.

How can we stop being subject to the whims of the people around us?

We are alive in Christ, and dead to sin, and raised with Christ—and we are also seated with him!

Ephesians 1 tells us that God "raised Him from the dead and seated Him at His right hand in the heavenly *places*, far above all rule and authority and power and dominion.... And He put all things in subjection under His feet."[1]

---

1. From Ephesians 1:20-23 (NASB)

Jesus is above all the spiritual forces.

And then this is what he does for us: "God raised us up with Christ and seated us with him in the heavenly realms in Christ Jesus."[2]

We are seated with Christ.

Which means that we, too, are above all the spiritual forces, above the "rule and authority and power and dominion."

We don't have to participate in the grumpiness from our position, seated in the heavenlies, above the spiritual forces. Above the grumpiness!

***

Lord Jesus! Thank you for your truth! Thank you that you sat down when you finished your work. Thank you that you are seated in heavenly places, and that we are seated in heavenly places with Christ.

Teach us what it means to live from that reality. Thank you, Lord.

---

2. Ephesians 2:6

Chapter Twenty-Three

GIVE ME YOUR ASHES

The great exchange of Isaiah 61:3: "to bestow on them a crown of beauty instead of ashes, the oil of joy instead of mourning, and a garment of praise instead of a spirit of despair."

The Lord said to Kris Vallotton, "Give me your ashes."[1]

And Kris said, "What are you talking about? I don't have any ashes! I'm from a strong faith movement! We focus on hope! We get our breakthrough even before the problem comes!"

And the Lord paused his protest.

Son, in the last few months, you've lost one of your closest friends after a valiant 18-month

---

1. From two nearly identical messages, based on two different talks, called "Give Me Your Ashes," Parts 1 and 2, September 15 and 22, 2022.

struggle with cancer. Give me your ashes.

Son, you've gone through several years of extremely difficult decisions, trying to navigate the challenges of governing and leading a body in that's prominent body in a city, where the city is making specific demands, and after 22 years of building relationships, you don't want to overthrow that trust-building. But it's hard for the congregation to understand. You have no way to please everyone all the time. Son, give me your ashes.

You've been talking about retirement for the last year, not because you think that that's what I am calling you to, but because you're carrying so much pain, you're looking for a way out. Give me your ashes.

This conversation went on for a while.

God gives beauty for ashes, not beauty for nothing.

Kris said, "If we don't give him our ashes, we're going to get an ash heap. Then everything that we see, everything that we taste, everything that we touch, everything that we smell, becomes filtered through these ashes."

In his message, Kris asked the listeners to make a cup with our hands and hold them in front of us, and think about the different ashes we carry.

Then hand them to Jesus. "I don't want them. Please make something beautiful out of them."

After we prayed that prayer once, the Lord often continues to bring up different memories.

"Here's another pocket of ashes. Do you want to give those ones to me, too?"

"Yes, thank you, Jesus. I do."

***

Thank you, Lord, that "Blessed are those who mourn, for they shall be comforted." We can walk through mourning with you.

Jesus, as we put give these ashes to you, please take them and make them beautiful.

Come and wipe us clean the from any of the residue.

Wash out our eyes, wipe out our ears, brush off our hair.

Clean us off from this sense of the ashes of our lives coating us.

Lord, we want to be covered and clean with you. Thank you, Jesus. Amen.

Chapter Twenty-Four

IF YOU HAVEN'T GOT YOUR HEALTH ...

Prince Humperdinck: I've got my country's five hundredth anniversary to plan, my wedding to arrange, my wife to murder, and Guilder to frame for it. I'm swamped.

Count Rugen: Get some rest. If you haven't got your health, you haven't got anything.[1]

While Count Rugen should not be the final say on health, of course the physical body matters. If we aren't in good health, it's difficult to think about much else.

---

1. From *The Princess Bride*

Cindy McFaden learned this prayer from the late Pastor Jack Hayford.

Body, line up under my soul.

Soul, line up under my spirit.

Spirit, line up under the Holy Spirit.

The body, in alignment, should be under the soul, often defined as the mind, will, memories, and emotions.

The soul should be under the spirit, which is the essential you, the God-breathed part of you.

And the essential you, of course, should be under the Holy Spirit, under his guidance and leading.

***

Lord, Genesis tells us, "The LORD God took the man and put him in the Garden of Eden to work it and take care of it."[2]

You invite us to cultivate and watch over your good creation.

In order for us to do that well, we need to be in proper alignment, and so we speak to ourselves:

Body, line up under my soul.

Soul, line up under my spirit.

Spirit, line up under the Holy Spirit.

Amen.

2. Genesis 2:15

CHAPTER TWENTY-FIVE

A STORY OF SMOLDERING WICKS

A my tells this story of progressive breakthrough prayer.

***

A client called one day. "I don't know what's happening, but everything feels out of control. I'm praying, but I don't know if I'm just not going far enough?"

"Let's pray about, so we can get wisdom to know what direction we need to take."

In truth, I didn't feel qualified to pray at that moment. If anything, I felt like I needed prayer for some of the exact same things. I'd taken three short naps because of bone weariness, and struggled with discouragement and negative thoughts all day.

I, too, had prayed, but not much seemed to shift.

Lord, if this is only a situation in the practical, where starting new routines is actually discombobulating, that's fine.

But to any spirit of discouragement, I bind you, in the name of Jesus, and send you to him.

And, Lord, in the place of discouragement, I ask for a greater measure of joy.

And spirit of chaos! I rebuke you and bind you, in the name of Jesus. Go directly to him and do what he tells you.

In the place of chaos, I ask for the promise of the Holy Spirit: power, love, and a sound mind.

The early Christians expected to do many exorcisms. Because they lived in a pagan society, they expected that new believers would have many things clinging to them that needed to be driven off.

Then as the believers were walking with God, they might picked up some unwanted spiritual cling-ons, some parasites, that needed to be removed for full health.

Spiritual healing or cleansing isn't once-and-done!

Lord, we have both been believing and telling ourselves lies, and cursing ourselves. Rather than believing that we are loved children of God, children Jesus came to die for, we're making our self-worth about how well we can do things.

In the name of Jesus Christ, and by his authority, cut us free from every one of those curses and lies. Lord, we want no part of lies, but only truth. We ask that you would renew our minds, give us the mind of Christ, so that we could look at ourselves as you see us.

For so many years, I hadn't realized that I could curse myself by saying something like, "I don't manage my time well," or "I'm a bad homeschooler"—these can *feel* true. But they're not true!

While it is true that I am absolutely not a perfect time manager or homeschooler, perfection is not a human quality, any more than purple skin.

If I've put myself under a curse, I need to pray to cut it off.

What freedom comes from cutting free!

Lord, I rebuke the spirit of mischief, the spirit of contention. I bind you and send you to Jesus to do with as he will.

In place of these, I ask you to send us more of the fruit of your Holy Spirit: love, joy, peace, patience, kindness, goodness, faithfulness, and self-control.

I love the insight that after bad things leave, you need to fill the empty places with good things.

Tired of fighting? Bind and cast out the spirit of fighting, and replace it with peace.

Ready for your mind to stop accusing you? Bind and cast out the accuser, cover yourself with the blood of Christ, and thank God for the love he has shown to you.

Thank you, God, that you are kinder than we are to ourselves. We remember our sins, but you have forgotten them.

I bind the spirit of weariness, this unnatural tiredness that does not come from you. Go to Jesus and do what he tells you.

Lord, you say that you give to your beloved rest. I know that isn't definitional—that if we happen to wake in the night, that doesn't mean that we're not your beloved. But rest is a gift you give.

And if you choose not to give it, Lord, I ask that you would show us how to use those middle-of-the-night hours wisely, and that you would multiply every minute we do sleep, until we're fully rested.

We both left this time of prayer feeling renewed.

It was said of Jesus that he wouldn't snuff out a smoldering wick. We might update that today to, "A smoking match he will not quench."

At the start of the prayer, we felt like burned out matches, with just a bit of smoke coming off.

And Jesus came and blew on the exhausted parts until the fire flared again.

Thanks be to God who, in less than a half hour, can restore the weary and encourage the weak.

***

Lord, release our voices. Release our tongues to speak your words, to pray your words, to move in power in this earth.

Lord, your word says that there is no fear in love, but perfect love casts out fear.

It also says that you have not given us a spirit of fear, but you've given us one of power, love, and a sound mind.

So Lord God, we bind any spirit of fear. We send it to Jesus for him to deal with. And in the place of that, Lord, bless us with the power, love, and sound mind that you promise.

Thank you, Lord, that you are not a man that you should lie.

We bring you into remembrance that this is actually your nature and your character. We are so thankful that this is what you choose to do, to heal and to move on our behalf.

CHAPTER TWENTY-SIX

FRUIT THAT REMAINS

D uring the Last Supper, Jesus said to his disciples, "You did not choose me, but I chose you and appointed you so that you might go and bear fruit—fruit that will last—and so that whatever you ask in my name the Father will give you."[1]

We, too, want our lives to bear lasting fruit.

On the one hand, we recognize that, no matter what we do with our days, our fruitfulness comes in walking with the Spirit.

We can love others, show compassion, exercise self-control, and so on, whether the tasks we do make any difference in the world.

On the other hand ... we want our work to matter. In *The Lean Startup*, Eric Ries talks about the pain of writing code for

---

1. John 15:16

six months that needed to be discarded as soon as it was done, because it wasn't useful to the company.

Thought leader Sam Woods talked about how all his work for the previous three years was sunsetting soon, due to shifts in the computer world.

Marketers and authors know the pain of writing an article or a novel that never gets read.

Evangelists and teachers know the grief of speaking and teaching to an audience that doesn't receive the good news.

We want fruit that remains.

***

Lord, Paul wrote, "Therefore, my dear brothers and sisters, stand firm. Let nothing move you. Always give yourselves fully to the work of the Lord, because you know that your labor in the Lord is not in vain."[2]

We don't want to work in vain.

Lord, we also think of the words of the Psalmist: "Unless the Lord builds the house, the builders labor in vain. Unless the Lord watches over the city, the guards stand watch in vain. In vain you rise early and stay up late, toiling for food to eat—for he grants sleep to those he loves."[3]

---

2. 1 Corinthians 15:58

3. Psalm 127:1-2

Please build the house, Lord. We don't want to work in vain. We want lasting fruit.

Thank you, though, that as Paul wrote to the church at Philippi, "But even if I am being poured out like a drink offering on the sacrifice and service coming from your faith, I am glad and rejoice with all of you."[4]

If the work of our hands makes no immediate difference, and we are poured out like a drink offering, that, too, can be a beautiful offering to you.

Thank you, Lord, that in your kingdom, we have no way to lose. Amen.

---

4. Philippians 2:17

CHAPTER TWENTY-SEVEN

THE GOD OF ABUNDANCE

J esus had a lot to say and demonstrate about abundance.
Although we might think of Jesus as a sort of homeless
wanderer, he really wasn't poor. He could create food and
wine apparently at will, and call forth a fish with a gold coin
in its mouth.

In John 21, seven disciples had gone fishing, but they caught
nothing.

> Early in the morning, Jesus stood on the shore,
> but the disciples did not realize that it was Jesus.
> He called out to them, "Friends, haven't you any
> fish?"
> "No," they answered.
> He said, "Throw your net on the right side of
> the boat and you will find some." When they did,

they were unable to haul the net in because of the large number of fish.

Then the disciple whom Jesus loved said to Peter, "It is the Lord!"

Kris Vallotton, in teaching on the last chapter of John, pointed out that, when the disciples cast out their nets and couldn't haul them in because they were so full, that bounty, that abundance, that over-the-top provision was the sign to John that Jesus was the one who spoke to them.

Jesus didn't give them directions so they could catch two small fish. John didn't say, "Oh! Here's a minnow, so at least we won't starve. Must be the Lord."

No. Jesus' abundant provision revealed his presence.

John recognized Jesus because of the abundance of the catch. The nets-so-full-they-had-to-tow-them: that was the sign that Jesus was in their midst.

When they landed, they saw a fire of burning coals there with fish on it, and some bread. Jesus said to them, "Bring some of the fish you have just caught."

So Simon Peter climbed back into the boat and dragged the net ashore. It was full of large fish, 153, but even with so many the net was not torn.

Jesus said to them, "Come and have breakfast."

Jesus didn't say to them, "Thanks so much for catching all those fish. I'm pretty hungry. Why don't you make me breakfast?"

No! He was already preparing breakfast for them.

They simply had to come and eat, surrounded by 153 large fish, their companions, and Jesus.

Of course, not every season of life feels like it is stuffed to bursting with abundance. The disciples themselves had just come through some pretty horrific days, between losing Jesus, the confusion of the resurrection, and the fact that he was no longer daily with them.

But what a statement of John's, that when he saw abundance, he knew: "It is the Lord!"

***

Lord, your word says in Psalm 84:11, "For the LORD God is a sun and shield; the LORD bestows favor and honor; no good thing does he withhold from those whose walk is blameless."

You say, Lord, that you give us favor and honor, and that you withhold no good thing.

Thank you for being our sun and our shield, the source of our light and heat, as well as our protection. Thank you that you demonstrate the heart of God, to bless and provide.

Lord, for any way that our souls feel a pinch right now; for any way that you do not seem to be pouring out abundance; for any way that life might feel like the fishing-all-night-with-no-catch

... Lord, call out the next instructions, so that our nets might be full.

Lord, may we would have a sense of you as the plentiful, abundant God that you are.

In Jesus' holy name, and for the praise of his glory, amen.

CHAPTER TWENTY-EIGHT

THE RIGHT TIME

"To every thing there is a season, and a time to every purpose under the heaven."[1]

Workplace Prayer client Shane said, "I have a little prayer that I've prayed for years."

God bring us the right clients,
God bring us the right employees,
God bring us the right revenue,
At the right time.

He said,

There's a time and season for everything.

There's a right quantity of income. Too little impedes your growth. Too much tends toward quick expansion that could end up smothering you, if you don't have your systems in place.

---

1. Ecclesiastes 3:1 (KJV)

The right employees make the owner's life easier,
and they serve the clients well.
And the right clients make life a joy.

Shane prays for the clients and employees to be drawn, at the right time, like magnets, to his business.

***

God bring us the right clients,
  God bring us the right employees,
  God bring us the right revenue,
  At the right time.
  Amen.

CHAPTER TWENTY-NINE

THE FAVOR AND BEAUTY OF THE LORD

The only Psalm attributed to Moses, Psalm 90, ends with this beautiful verse: "May the favor of the Lord our God rest on us; establish the work of our hands for us—yes, establish the work of our hands."[1]

Favor, by definition: "approval, support, or liking for someone or something; overgenerous preferential treatment; an act of kindness beyond what is due or usual."

Already lovely.

But the word in the Hebrew, *no'-am*, can also be translated "beauty": "let the beauty of the LORD our God be upon us."

---

1. Psalm 90:17

Let the agreeableness, kindness, pleasantness, delightful-ness, suitableness, splendor or grace—the beauty or fa-vor—rest upon us.[2]

It's the same word found in Psalm 27:4: "One *thing* have I desired of the LORD, that will I seek after; that I may dwell in the house of the LORD all the days of my life, to behold the **beauty** of the LORD, and to enquire in his temple."[3]

Moses asked not just that he get preferential treatment.

He asked that the splendor and grace of God rest on him.

The same splendor or grace that David would have happily gazed upon, all the days of his life.

May *this* glory rest upon us.

Astonishing. Beautiful.

In addition, the scriptures repeat something for emphasis.

When Jesus said, "Truly, truly, I say unto you,"[4] he wasn't demonstrating a nervous tic, or offering the equivalent of extended throat-clearing. And of course he wasn't saying, "Everything else I've been saying was a lie, but now I'm telling the truth."

No. He was saying, "Seriously: pay attention."

---

2. https://www.blueletterbible.org/lexicon/h5278/kjv/wlc/0-1/

3. KJV

4. John 5:24 and elsewhere

In the Old Testament, the prophet Isaiah wrote, "You will keep in perfect peace those whose minds are steadfast, because they trust in you."[5]

"Perfect peace" in the Hebrew is *shalom shalom*. Peace peace. Wellness and wholeness, doubled.

Moses, then, when he wanted to ask for his works to be established, doubled the entire phrase: "establish the work of our hands for us—yes, establish the work of our hands."

***

Lord, we want our work to be established. Fully and completely.

Make our work firm, fixed, stable.

May it be secure, enduring, directed aright, steadfast.

Prepare it, arrange it, settle it.

Provide for it, direct it, order it.

We want our work to be accomplished and remain.

---

5. Isaiah 26:3

CHAPTER THIRTY

THE BLESSING OF GOD

G od gave this beautiful blessing to Aaron.[1]

The Lord bless you, and keep you [protect you, sustain you, and guard you];
The Lord make His face shine upon you [with favor],
And be gracious to you [surrounding you with lovingkindness];

The Lord lift up His countenance (face) upon you [with divine approval],
And give you peace [a tranquil heart and life].

---

1. Number 6:24-26 (AMP)

***

Thank you, God, that you instituted blessings, and that you allow life to be in the tongue. Lord, so many of us have experienced the power of death in the tongue; please may we be people with life in our tongues.

Lord, may this blessing go forth, and rest on your people.

Lord, bless us indeed this week. Enlarge our influence. Let your hand would be on us. Keep us from the evil one.

We give you praise and glory. In the name of Jesus, amen.

CONCLUSION

The Old Testament offered prayer, not as a burden, but as a joy: "These I will bring to my holy mountain and give them joy in my house of prayer. Their burnt offerings and sacrifices will be accepted on my altar; for my house will be called a house of prayer for all nations."[1]

God gives joy in the house of prayer.

In the New Testament, when the disciples reported on some of their ministry adventures, Jesus suddenly had the most joyful moment of his earthly life: "At that time Jesus, full of joy through the Holy Spirit, said, 'I praise you, Father, Lord of heaven and earth, because you have hidden these things from the wise and learned, and revealed them to little children. Yes, Father, for this is what you were pleased to do.'"[2]

The work of the kingdom brings joy.

---

1. Isaiah 56:7

2. Luke 10:21

Our prayer for you is that you will remember to pray for the work of your hands, and that, as you do, you will have supernatural wisdom and insight, restored relationships, hope, abundance ... and joy.

BONUS OPTION: TAKE COMMUNION

Depending on your denomination, you may not be comfortable taking communion apart from the larger body of Christ.

If this does not bother your conscience, though, we encourage you to proclaim the Lord's death until he comes ... regularly! Maybe even daily.

Here's a reading to accompany communion.

***

Faithfulness and the First Communion

Lord, we think of the first communion, and how you gave the bread and the wine to your disciples, knowing that that very night, one would betray you, one would deny you, and the other ten would turn away.

We think of how John records that, after eating, the disciples began disputing about which of them was the greatest.

These were the men who partook of the first Lord's Table.

And you invited them to fellowship.

Lord Jesus, thank you that you don't look on our worthiness to determine whether we can partake or not. Thank you that you don't deal with us according to our faithfulness. "If we are faithless, he remains faithful, for he cannot disown himself" (II Timothy 2:13).

Thank you, Jesus, for how beautiful you are.

***

For I received from the Lord what I also passed on to you: The Lord Jesus, on the night he was betrayed, took bread, and when he had given thanks, he broke it and said, "This is my body, which is for you; do this in remembrance of me." In the same way, after supper he took the cup, saying, "This cup is the new covenant in my blood; do this, whenever you drink it, in remembrance of me." For whenever you eat this bread and drink this cup, you proclaim the Lord's death until he comes (I Corinthians 11:23-26 NIV).

***

Thank you, Lord, for the power of the Table of the Lord. Thank you for the amazing covenant you've made with us.

Lord, it gives us such hope. It gives us such joy.

Thank you for the new covenant. Thank you for your body. Thank you for your blood. Thank you for the bread, and thank you for the cup.

We eat and drink, in Jesus' name.

Amen.

Let's celebrate![1]

---

1. Taken from *Savor Communion*, by the authors, which includes a month's worth of readings, like this one, to facilitate communion.

An Invitation

At Workplace Prayer, we experiment in prayer as we pray for businesses, and the people and families behind the work.

We invite you to be a part.

Find out more at workplaceprayer.com, or email connect@ workplaceprayer.com for more information.

ABOUT THE AUTHORS

Dr. **Amy Lykosh** is an author, mentor, and entrepreneur. Through Workplace Prayer, Makarios Press, the Make Prayer Beautiful podcast, and more, she covers businesses in prayer and raises up intercessors to do the same. She lives outside Charlottesville, Virginia with her husband and five sons.

Enjoy the Prayer Refresh: 21 short prayers to pray as you go about your day. praybig.me/refresh

***

Dr. Bob Perry, a self-described "fasting intercessor," has been a student of prayer for four decades. He constantly seeks to hone his craft, studying not only how people pray around the globe and throughout history, but also constantly asking, "Lord, teach me to pray." He lives in East Nashville, Tennessee with his wife, and enjoys spending time with his four adult children.

He has led multiple prayer initiatives that have trained and mobilized hundreds of thousands of people in prayer. An author and coach, currently he serves the business community, praying for business owners in every sphere of influence.

Find him at workplaceprayer.com.

Made in the USA
Middletown, DE
11 August 2025

Our Favorite Prayers for Business

Over the last five years, the Workplace Prayer team has experimented with prayers for business.

What prayers seem most effective?

What prayers are so powerful that we notice if we skip them?

How do we pray, morning, day, and night, without burning out?

It is our pleasure to bring you these thirty favorite prayers as an overview.

Big picture, "Thy Kingdom come" prayers; appropriate warfare prayers; prayers from the scripture; prayers from the saints.

Thank you for your interest in praying for businesses—we are excited for you to enjoy the best of what we've found across tens of thousands of hours.

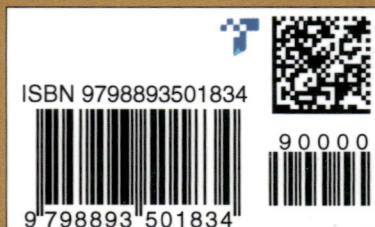

ISBN 9798893501834